Millionaire Success Habits

Discover The Daily Strategies That Make and Keep The Wealthy Rich (Money Mindsets, Success Ideas, Prosperity Rituals)

Alexander S. Presley

Millionaire Success Habits: Discover The Daily Strategies That Make and Keep The Wealthy Rich (Money Mindsets, Success Ideas, Prosperity Rituals)

This book was self-published with the amazing help of Self-Publishing Made Easy Now! [1] . You can grab a free copy of the checklist that started my journey here: FREE Self-Publishing Checklist [2] .

[1] https://selfpublishingmadeeasynow.com/xpjv

[2] https://selfpublishingmadeeasynow.com/free_checklist

Table of Contents

1 - Introduction...6

2 - The Habit Habit...9

    Habits and how we get them...........................9

    What does it take to "learn" a new habit?.....11

3 - The Passion Habit.......................................14

    How can passion be a habit?.........................14

    Passion sizzling inside us.............................14

    Is there money in my passion?....................16

4 - Part I – Habits to have to try figuring out what it is......18

    Habit 1...19

    Habit 2...19

    Habit 3...20

    Habit 4...20

5 - Part II – Habits to have in your current job.............22

6 - Habits with Your Game Plan.....................25

    Write your goals down.................................25

    Think long term...28

    Take Inventory...29

    Don't entertain self-doubt and fear or taking risks.................30

    Keep a Positive Mental Attitude (PMA)....................32

7 - Habits for the Brain....................................34

    Don't stop learning and studying.................34

    They read and read everyday......................35

    Be financially educated...............................37

    Learn from people's failures.......................37

    Accept and embrace change.......................38

    Take a few minutes per day to "just think" and clear your mind 40

    Simplify, and be judicious with your words....................40

8 - Habits with Your Body...............................43

    The Sweat Habits..44

    Millionaires rise and shine early!................44

Ask questions..46

Listen more and talk less..47

Don't procrastinate and avoid "time wasters"............48

Make decisions and quickly..50

Never mention the words, "bad luck" when it comes to results 52

Do not blame others...53

Compete Only With Yourself...53

Control your emotions, and once again, PMA!............54

Review your performance each night...........................55

9 - Habits with Your Pocketbook...........................57

Pay yourself first..57

Don't spend what you don't have..................................58

Try to avoid personal credit as much as you can.......61

Create multiple streams of income...............................63

Invest and invest wisely - don't let the money sit around..........64

Share Your Millions..66

Habits with Your Networks and People.......................68

Consider yourself a brand and make yourself into one............70

10 - So what do you do to build a personal brand?.............73

Find a mentor..74

Consider advice and information from anyone............76

Associate with successful people, and avoid toxic people..........77

Invest resources in productive and success-oriented people.....79

11 - Habits with your Communications and Technology.....81

Start a blog or a website..82

12 - Audit your online presence.............................85

13 - Conclusion...87

Create the success process...87

Do not fear failure and criticism..................................88

Erase all doubt..89

Be congruent and consistent...89

Become a master...90

Go above and beyond!..90

Thank You...92

Disclaimer..93

1 - Introduction

The Spectrem Group, a research firm that specializes in wealthy investors, concluded a study in 2016 that showed that 10 million households in the United States had assets of over $1 million or greater, aside from their homes.

The study also showed that there were close to 11 million millionaires in the United States through the end of 2015. This means that less than 5% of individuals in the country can call themselves millionaires, which in the eyes of most, represents success the good old American way.

When we mention of millionaire "success stories" today, most people conjure up images of internet magnates like Facebook's Mark Zuckerberg or Amazon's Jeff Bezos. Five years ago, a millionaire (or billionaire) whiz meant Microsoft's Bill Gates and Apple's Steve Jobs.

If we further step back just a generation, we would have been talking about the success stories of Walmart's Sam Walton and McDonald's Ray Kroc. There are thousands of millionaire success stories in all shapes and sizes in the United States - in all fields, in every city, and in every state.

They could be driving down the 405 freeway in Los Angeles

in a Silver Bentley, or in a beat-up station wagon on an Arkansas dirt road.

A millionaire success story can also be a wired Gary Vaynerchuk tittering and gesticulating wildly in front of a rapt crowd of thousands, or it could be Carly Fiorina, who started out as a quiet pseudo secretary before joining Hewlett-Packard and becoming its CEO on her way to become a presidential candidate.

Success could be Uncle Warren (Buffet) shaking up the Twitterers with an off-the-cuff stock suggestion, or a plain old uncle Warren scaring up a steak at your Memorial Day barbecue.

Consider millionaire Oprah, millionaire Donald, millionaire Lebron, millionaire Rhianna, and the Millionaire Next Door. Some of them are much more "millionaire" than the rest, but millionaires nevertheless. In a capitalist country like the United States, nothing spells success more than the eleven letters that spell out millionaire.

Millionaires have been probed, studied, and poked into unlike any other segment of society. One could complain that politicians and movie stars have been subject to more scrutiny. But– they are all millionaires also anyway, so they get to be in our millionaire subset.

Millionaires also share many traits and habits that have financially separated them from at least 9/10th of the population. If they didn't flat out inherit, steal, or drug-push their way to these millions, they certainly did a lot of things that regular folk didn't do and possess something most others apparently do not have.

In this book, we will learn what drives successful millionaires to the financial heights they have reached. We don't go into demographics to establish possible cultural or age profiles, because it doesn't seem to matter if you're 18 or 80, black or white, Chinese or Caucasian.

We will instead talk about how they got to where they are doing specific things that anybody can do. Success habits are universal, and anyone can avail of the toolkit that is this book. Many say that if you want to become a millionaire, it doesn't hurt to start thinking like one. I say you need to start acting like one. The voyage to millions is about mind and action.

Bon Voyage!

2 - The Habit Habit

Habits and how we get them

Imagine waking up in the morning – you shuffle to the bathroom, stare into the mirror, and pull off a post-it that you placed there the night before. On this note is a list of things you need to accomplish before you even get ready for work: Brush your teeth, wash your face, take a shower, shave (both men and women!), and even take a tinkle.

Now, wait a minute - You don't need to list these things down in the first place! These are things that you've been doing all your life practically on auto pilot. We do a lot of these things without even giving them a second thought, and in the case of these early morning bathroom tasks, we can even do them half-asleep.

We are doing these things because they are habits. Most dictionaries define habit as, "a settled or regular tendency or practice, especially one that is hard to give up."

We know that a habit is regular, because we do some tasks on a regular basis, from our bathroom tasks to our habit of regular oil-changes, to making sure we check that all the doors are locked before we call it a night. By definition a habit is also settled. How did brushing our teeth get "settled?" Consider how you got started brushing your teeth.

I doubt it was a pleasant experience. Your mom or dad probably got you to stand up on stool when you were 3 or 4 years old and made to put this gooey stuff in your mouth and rub it up and down your gums vigorously.

The process to acquire this habit, as it is with other habits wasn't exactly a walk in the park, but with repetition and the constant reminder that the habit was good for you, the action "settled" as part of your regular routine. You do it because it's good for you, and knowledgeable and respected people gave you sage advice on its benefits, and in the case of your teeth, mechanics.

NBA basketball player Stephen Curry makes it a habit to shoot at least 200 shots every day, with either hand during the basketball season. Have you ever tried doing this? It is a mind-numbing and elbow-numbing couple of hours.

Pain or no pain, this habit has made him one of the most successful athletes in the history of sports, never mind basketball. In 2017, he signed the biggest sports contract in team sports history at the time, over 200 million dollars.

So we know what a habit is – A little act that you do every day that becomes a part of your being, almost like an extra limb that is an extension of your personality and existence.

What does it take to "learn" a new habit?

If you decided to develop a positive millionaire habit, how long would it take you to develop them? A team of researchers at University College London led by health psychologist Phillippa Lally embarked on a lengthy study to find out exactly that.

Over a period of 3 months, they observed the behavior of almost 100 subjects to determine if it was possible to arrive at a number. Lally's research revealed that it took on the average, 66 days or just over two months to "acquire" a new habit.

One thing that successful people will tell us is to remember that there is no such thing as an overnight success. Scientists may have come up with a magical 66-day number, but this should by no means tell you that you have a punishing deadline, or if you're an eternal optimist, may consider that the 66 days is more than enough time to be successful.

The key to being a millionaire success is to realize that there are no shortcuts to success, and some have actually taken "long-cuts" to get to where they are.

We need to return to the definition again of habit again, and let's talk a little bit about the last part: a habit is "hard to give up." Consider the power of that group of words. When we have been brushing our teeth all our lives, we know after some time that we can't stop cold turkey and leave our teeth to the elements.

The alternatives are cavities, toothaches, and worst having to get a tooth pulled. Same with changing our car's oil – not doing so can cause thousands of dollars in repairs. What does this tell us about stopping good habits? There are CONSEQUENCES that can be serious.

When we acquire a good habit, we can get significant benefits from that habit. We know that if we skip a day without doing it, or worse, drop the habit altogether, there could be some pretty dire consequences.

W.H. Auden, the literary giant once said, "Routine, in an intelligent man, is a sign of ambition." Ambition is undoubtedly a foundation of success; but probably more important than ambition is what good habits can do for you as a human being.

Habits define your personality, and your personality reflects your character. Your character may eventually become your number one selling point, so a foundation of excellent habits is your key to success.

When desiring success, the correct habits are essential to the pursuit. Probably the biggest key to excellence is loving what you are doing. There is no sense putting together 66-day habit adventures if you can't get up for what you are doing anyway.

3 - The Passion Habit

How can passion be a habit?

Passion isn't a habit, you might say, so how does it get ink on a book about habits?

First, the right habits applied to passion has meant success for thousands of people since we started tracking the lives of millionaires.

Second, we can use habits to not only figure out what our passion is but also to fan the flames of that passion to keep it burning.

Passion sizzling inside us

If you ask any successful millionaire why he or she got to where she was going, among the first things they would say would be something like, "I really liked what I was doing."

Director Steven Spielberg as a young teenager in Los Angeles loved to hang around the Universal Studios lot, convincing the guards to let him in and watch the filming of major movie projects. But even before this, he had a hand-held camera as a young boy and even produced a two-hour movie "Firelight". It was always his passion to make films.

Spielberg is but one of the many documented cases of a person's passion taking over someone's life. Steve Jobs liked fooling around with electronics and led to Apple, and the world's greatest retailers like Sam Walton started lemonade stands when they started barely learned how to ride a bicycle.

To these entrepreneurs, exchanging goods for money became addictive, and they just didn't stop until it was physically impossible to do so. Their passion became their reason for living, and everything else took a backseat.

This passion ethic is most often expressed in the catchphrase, "My job doesn't feel like work at all." Successful millionaires and millionaires-to-be jump up from bed in the morning raring to work on their passion, and sometimes do not know when to stop even while already working late into the night.

This passion is not reserved for the documented rich and famous, however. I am sure you have heard of successful doctors who were carrying toy stethoscopes all over the place even before they were old enough to go to school, or a 3-year old would-be rocket scientist already trying to figure out ways to launch a wood and cardboard projectile from their backyard into outer space

This passion is apparent because THEY PURSUE THINGS THAT INTEREST THEM. This passion is like a fire burning in their heart when they go to bed at night, and a fire under their behinds when they get up in the morning.

They just need to get up and go and do whatever it is that they love the most. The maverick writer and journalist Hunter S. Thompson said it best: "Anything that gets your blood racing is probably worth doing."

Is there money in my passion?

This is a book about millionaire success, so now that you know what your passion is, are you able to monetize this? Most experts would agree and say yes, anything can be a lucrative effort if you put your mind and sweat into it. If you do something you love to do, and do it really, really, well, there is very little doubt that you can make a living out of it.

In her book, "Do What You Love, the Money Will Follow," author Marsha Sinetar maintains that if you've found what you really like to do in life, you can expect the compensation to come somewhere down the road.

With technology leaping ahead at a pace beyond what most people can catch up with, monetizing may actually be faster and cheaper now. With the internet and automation, it is cheaper to market and sell today. You can have a wider reach with less investment. The Habits with Technology chapter will bring much more enlightenment on this.

But what if I don't know my passion?

4 - Part I – Habits to have to try figuring out what it is

Passion for his interests started way early for Elon Musk, the billionaire owner of Tesla cars, and soon to be pioneer of tourism outer space flights. He sold his first video game when he was 12, and was a science fiction addict when he was much younger. If you are not a Musk or Spielberg, what is your shot at millionaire success if you don't even know what it is you are passionate about?

Your true passion may be discovered in little increments, with possible little side interests unfolding themselves slowly. In reality, most psychologists have concluded that that a majority of people do not possess that one overwhelming and all-consuming passion. Many people actually have multiple passions unlike the prodigies that have frequently read about.

Multiple passions are healthy because this means that a person is well-rounded with varying interests. Someone for example, may have a passion for playing the guitar and a passion for doing accounting work. Together, or individually these passions may not lead to millionaire success as the next great singing C.P.A., but there are other ways that financial success can still be had.

Still, you may possibly find out in 66 days if you want to make it a habit of trying to find out what you really want to do. Here are some things that you can do for the next 66 days and figure out if there is some passion burning deep inside you that is ready to burst forth from within.

Habit 1

Ask yourself these three questions every day for 66 days— (1) What can I do for at least three years without getting paid, and not complain about it? (2) What can I read dozens of books about without having to put it down without yawning or falling asleep? (3) What would I prefer to be doing with my time if finances were not a consideration?

Habit 2

List down the top 10 things you would NOT do, even if your life depended on it. A good place to start is to list down 10 jobs you wouldn't take on. If you're an entrepreneur, list down 10 products or services that you wouldn't sell. Look at this list, and update it for the next 66 days,

Habit 3

List down the things that you suck at, and conversely list down the things that you are good at, and review this list every day for the next 66 days, This does not mean you are looking to eliminate certain things, but it will focus your mind on possible areas of passion.

For example, you could be horrible at golf, but there may be something about the game that will drive your passion – you can blog on the best golf courses for average or below average players, or even write about, and even sell golf equipment that can cater to players like you.

Habit 4

Turn on your memory banks, and try to remember: What did you LOVE doing as a child? Like Elon Musk, did you love to read science fiction? Did you really enjoy your foray into the lemonade stand business?

Practicing these habits may not yield any direct results, but it will get you started thinking about what burns deep inside you. There probably isn't a eureka moment that will light up in your head, but you have started an active process to figure out what your passion is. This is light years ahead of where you were before you picked up this book.

It is not wrong to not have a single burning passion. For the meantime, if we are "stuck" in an 8-5 job, there are still ways to have successful habits on the way to millions.

But what if I don't know my passion?

5 - Part II – Habits to have in your current job

What happens if after months trying to figure out what your passion is, you still end up with Big Fat Zero? Does it mean that you get to be stuck in your crappy office for the rest of your days? The honest answer is yes, maybe. Remember however, that you are trying to be a millionaire success, and not necessarily the next Sam Walton or Richard Branson.

What is wrong with a job anyway? Most people really like to be employees if only for financial stability and income and career security. So what if you are stuck in a J.O.B?" (Just Over Broke, as they say).

There are many "dreamers" in offices all over the United States that go about their work as if one day, the "big break" will come and that they will walk out of their offices triumphantly as millionaires with no further use for their employer.

Contrast this laid back ethic with that of a Michael Ovitz, the former CEO of Disney, who didn't sit around dreaming big, but just decided that he was going the be the best messenger boy in the basement of an artists' agency in Los

Angeles.

Then there is Ms. Fiorina again, who figured that she should be the best receptionist she could possibly be before becoming the first female CEO of a tech company in the United States.

You become more millionaire ready if you have an accurate mindfulness that you have really no idea what your real passion is, and proceed to work your behind off like Michael Ovitz and Carly Fiorina. The alternative is to have a misplaced confidence in a false passion and wait for that clock to hit 5:00 so you can go home and do more daydreaming.

If you have a hard time figuring out what your passion is, consider these passion habits:

- List down things that you like about your job, about the people that you like, and about the company that you work for. You could end up being passionate about what you're doing, end up working harder than anyone and end up creating your own ladder to the top.

- Conversely, list down the things and people that you do not particularly care for. You have two choices on what to do with these: (1) Avoid them completely and craft run arounds so you can minimize your contact with them, or (2) Convert the negative into something positive, like instead of ignoring an unrepentant sour puss of an office-mate, try to be nice to him or her with daily smiles and greetings. You'll never know.

You can work at a job and still become a millionaire if you exercise passion in your work. The job itself may not be your passion. But the passion in this case is the passion that you put in your job.

Getting good compensation in addition to getting constant recognition is almost a sure road to millionaire success. You may not make a feature film that will gross a billion dollars. or run Disney or Hewlett-Packard, but you can make your millionaire mark in other ways.

Armed with passion and the fire to pursue it, it is now to get on the doing.

6 - Habits with Your Game Plan

Millionaire passion is a fire that needs to be corralled and controlled. This control comes in the form of planning and goal setting. Before they hit the Big Time, millionaires didn't just step out of their houses and let the millions fall into their lap.

For most, the planning activity was treated by the would-be millionaires as a full-time job. For many, this was the most rigorous and mentally challenging phase of their millionaire trek.

If you want to be a millionaire, do as the successful ones did and do the following:

Write your goals down

Millionaires have vivid, limitless imaginations, so they can see their destination pretty clearly. Millionaires see their destination as having already happened, and they write them down. Passion will provide a destination, and writing down your goals will provide both a road map and a timetable to how do get to that destination.

A good addition to the goal setting exercise is to set and

visualize your dreams. This means that millionaires write down what their life would be like if they achieve their dreams such as living in a bigger house, drive nicer cars, go on luxury vacations, and taking care of their families.

The specific goals can then be written around these dreams. The "dreams" can also be a series of steps on a ladder, like milestones that need to be achieved. After you've made enough to buy your first dream, your Mercedes; your next step is the house by the beach, so you can now write down your goals for that dream.

Harvard University conducted a formal study of its graduates. They found out the 3% of graduates who wrote down their goals earned TEN times as much than those who didn't. When Comedian Jim Carrey was just starting out his career, he wrote himself a ten million dollar check, not knowing when and how he was going to get it.

All he knew was that he was going to earn the 10 mil from acting. He perfected his craft, applied for every acting gig that he could apply to, and worked his tail off. We all know where his career went.

Millionaires really do take their goals seriously by putting them down on paper. In the case of Jim Carrey, he kept the check in his wallet and looked at it many times a day until he actually accumulated that money and cashed the check. Many of the millionaires don't only leave the written goals sitting in their wallet or drawer.

Some actually write down their goals every single day. Some do this not because they want to change their goals. They do this so that they can adjust the way to get there, such coming up with new ideas, approaches, investments, and so forth.

Writing down your goals also aids in prioritizing your activities and your investments. You obviously want to place the most important things on the front burner and pour you resources on those.

You also select those activities that will yield the highest possible return first. Complete the $10,000 actions before you work the $100 ones. The quicker you complete the high return actions, the faster you will generate the money to your account. This is money-making efficiency.

These enhancements and adjustments can take the form of writing down weekly and even daily tasks, doing financial projections, or piling on new blocks on a burgeoning empire. Writing down your goals and refinements as a daily habit will provide you the extra push and momentum towards your millionaire destination.

Think long term

Millionaires are visionaries who do not think only about the present. They take a long-view of their businesses and careers, and set goals that span years, and even decades. They have looked way past the weeks and months of their business or career horizons. If you stretch your planning and goal setting as far as you can in the future, the wealthier you will become.

Millionaires do not think along the lines of, "I need to be able to pay my bills this month." Instead they think of things like, "I need to double revenues this fiscal year." Or instead of, "How do I get promoted each year for the next five years?"

Millionaires and the uber rich may seem impetuous and temperamental. They got to be that way because in the journey to success, they were actually very patient looking at the long-view.

Take Inventory

Having your passion and written goals in hand, an important habit to adopt is to be always aware what your current resources are. For the business millionaire, it might be essential to have adequate financing, and business infrastructure (manufacturing and retailing logistics, technology, storefront, web presence, etc.).

A precise knowledge of your market is also crucial, because you can end up having the best product with no one really to sell do.

If you are an employee about to volunteer for that once in a lifetime career-making project, a good place to start is to ask if you have the necessary skill set and knowledge. Also ask yourself if you will be able to satisfy the time commitment to pursue that special endeavor.

If you have a family, will you be able to give up weekends and holidays? Will you be able to withstand missing graduations, piano recitals, and football games of your kids?

Remember that to be a truly successful millionaire, you need your professional satisfaction to be congruent to your personal satisfaction. You should be able to mix business

with pleasure and risk losing things that are more important than making a buck or career success. Inventory your
time, lay out a graph showing the most crucial time phases,
and try to adjust this so that it doesn't destroy your personal
life.

Don't entertain self-doubt and fear or taking risks

It is not unusual for one's raging passion to get doused
when the realities of reading their goals on a piece of paper
or their tablet stare back at them. What is staring back is
monster eyes of theoretical impossibility, 22-hour work
days, undiscovered financing, and untouchable competition.

Everybody told Mark Zuckerberg that Facebook was already
been there done that, that there was no way he could get
financing to launch a maverick and untested social network.
People kept on telling Colonel Harland David Sander 69
years old, he could not possibly market fried chicken, no
matter how good his recipe was. At the young age of 72, he
launched what was to become the monster food empire,
KFC.

Millionaires did not waste their time thinking about how things could not get done. That is not how the successful ones think, and this fear attitude may be the hardest part about getting through the goal setting aspect of the road to millions.

Fear and doubt is ingrained in the human psyche. In the back of our heads, we worry about bills, tax returns, terrorist attacks, economic downturns, meteor strikes and alien invasions. We begin to doubt and fear everything as a matter of course.

This negativity trickles down into our innermost core, and turns into fear. Fear is an attitude, and attitude shifts are difficult, and the way to get bad attitudes shifted is to adopt habits to push past all the negativity. The biggest fear is the fear of failure, and this leads to risk avoidance. All the fear that has been embroiled in us has made us shun risk.

Business millionaires need to jump into the freezing waters of uncertainty even if there are no lifeboats to be seen for miles around. If you are employed, take on a project or a task that once seemed way beyond your skill set and experience level.

The worse than can possibly happen is that you get cut back

down to your original position, and getting extra marks for your initiative. You need to have a frame of mind that you will succeed. Discard negativity, and always be positive.

Keep a Positive Mental Attitude (PMA)

In her best-selling book, The Secret, Rhonda Byrne says that there is a Law of Attraction that the vibrations that we send out to the "Universe" are reflected back to us through the things that happen in our lives. If we send out positive vibrations, good things happen. If we sent out negative vibrations, then negativity ensues all over your life.

The Law of Attraction has been also "marketed" into various forms of PMA. There are thousands of books and posts about PMA and the overriding principle is that when something negative enters your mind, you should not only kick it out of your consciousness, but flip it 180 degrees and convert it to a positive thought.

For example, a negative thought might be, "I cannot get financing for this." Flip this into, "I can have many sources of money for this deal." Or, you can flip, "I cannot deliver this tough project to my bosses," to, "This is a piece of cake that I can deliver in no time."

PMA feeds your courage and commitment, and should be a big part of the millionaire process. Dale Carnegie, Napoleon Hill, and many other best-sellers use PMA as the cornerstone of their theories of success. There must be something right about PMA, so make it a daily habit ASAP.

You can't get to where you are going if you don't know where you are going. You should now put on your thinking cap and exercise your most important muscle embedded in your skull.

7 - Habits for the Brain

A millionaire's earning potential doesn't start with the enterprise or the job, it is mostly dictated by the mindset, and more particularly, the "BRAINset". You do not to be an Einstein with a Mensa I.Q. to be wildly successful, but this doesn't mean that you brain can remain stagnant while you are pumping out that next sale, working out that new contract, or finishing that new project in the office.

The worst attitude that you can have is to think that you know enough. You should never, ever stop learning. That's what Arnold Schwarzenegger exhorts, and he said this being in his sixties, having had a successful bodybuilding, movie, and political career. He never stops learning even after it looks like that he has reached the top of the heap in practically everything that he's ever tried.

The brain is the millionaire's most valuable tool, more than his bank account, his people, or his infrastructure. Doing things to make sure that this tool is sharpened and honed to tiptop toughness is job number one.

Don't stop learning and studying

The most successful businessmen, intellectuals, military giants, politicians, generals, etc. of history made sure they put aside time each day for study. Some millionaires, from all careers and persuasions have even gone to the length of either finishing their college credits, or pursued post graduate degrees. Education should not stop once you have earned your millions.

It didn't stop when you finished college either. If you don't continue learning, you will stagnate, just like a shark that stops swimming – it dies. Your brain, your enterprise, and career will die when you stop learning, because the world and competition continues to move. The following are prized habits to make sure learning is a lifelong experience.

They read and read everyday

If you walk into any millionaire's house, one of the most significant things that you might first notice is a ton of books, most likely even a private library. They know that learning through book reading does not stop when you get your diploma. Part of the formula for millionaire success is growing your skills and knowledge base.

A study once showed that about 85% of millionaires read at least two books each month. Their choices of books are not really about their business or their specialty. They read a lot about the biographies of successful people, careers, self-improvement, psychology, current events, and surprise surprise, leadership.

All it takes is just thirty minutes each day of reading, which 90% of successful millionaires do. Amazingly, you can learn a key concept or knowledge base in only a few hours when it took most people a ton of years to acquire.

This will set you apart from your peers because most people just do not like to read. Having a ton of specialized and general knowledge makes you more valuable to your customers, clients, co-workers, and bosses.

You can also be smart about managing your time during reading, Two-thirds of millionaires say that they listen to audio books while they are commuting, while only 10% that they read for entertainment purposes.

To stress the importance of reading, Facebook founder Mark Zuckerberg in 2015, started an internet reading club "A Year of Books". Those who joined committed to read at least two books per month, which they discussed on Facebook.

Be financially educated

Since you are interested in making millions, a good percentage of your time and even income, should go toward a financial education. Success is a process, the way out of the middle class is sweat, and financial knowledge will help you preserve your wealth.

If you have both in good amounts, you will make more money, and more importantly keep it. This is best done again, through books but many very high net worth millionaires hire expensive financial advisers to make sure that they are wisely invested.

Online brokerages like E*TRADE and TD Ameritrade not only accept online investments, but also have extensive research and education tools available online. You don't even have to invest in their portals to take advantage of many of the learning tools.

Learn from people's failures

While it is important to read and learn about successful people, it is just as important to learn from the failure of others. This may sound easy, but many people totally try to ignore other people's failures because it is not part of our nature to contemplate mistakes that were committed by others. This is also because we just don't believe that misfortunes that happen to other people cannot happen to us.

You may not find a lot of books devoted on this topic, but you can read about them in business magazines, newspapers, trade journals, and even word or mouth or third party testimonies.

The importance of this is obvious – you can avoid costly mistakes that others have already done. You don't need to have your product launch, job promotion, or bank account be the victim of a similar failure that has already happened to somebody else.

Accept and embrace change

Millionaires live in a world that is a dynamic system of moving parts. If you want to be safe, sit in an office chair doing the same thing in and out every day for a career. This is not necessarily bad, because many people are entirely comfortable with this situation, and that is why only 5% of Americans are millionaires.

The hallmark of a millionaire journey is the existence of bumps, rises, and uncertainties. Whether changes are big or small, these can be intimidating. Most people tend to fear change and are very insecure about losing their jobs, or missing a sale or a break from a vendor. This is because a vast majority of people just assume that change will be disruptive and terrifying.

Millionaires view these disruptions as opportunities, and rise to the challenge. Driving on the road, ordinary men feel big bumps on the road and either stop and move around those bumps. Millionaires drive right through them, confident that hitting a bump might propel them to even greater heights.

Most people change will be harmful most of the time, while successful millionaires look at any type of change, negative or positive, and are certain that these will actually be beneficial. For those just beginning on their millionaire journey, it is important to learn to welcome change together with the growth that comes along with it.

Doing so builds self-assurance and toughens you up for the longer road and bigger picture and goal. Confidence is important which is acquired by working hard, and by being prepared. Being prepared means having the proper tools to face whatever change will come along.

Take a few minutes per day to "just think" and clear your mind

You need to keep your brain wired and engaged for any reason daily. For fifteen minutes at the beginning or end of the day, think about anything at all to either relax or let go. It is almost like a personal barnstorming procedure, where you don't necessarily think about your business or job. The "agenda" can be about family, kids, relationships, health, and personal issues, among others.

These 15 minutes can even be in the form of some sort of meditative state just to totally clear the mind prepare it for the next round of intense millionaire mental exercises and activities.

Simplify, and be judicious with your words

While we talk about the right way to use your brain, a few words need to be said about what issues from the mouth. Our words reflect what our current thinking is, and many a ship has been sunk by ill-spoken thoughts.

You need to be cautious with both the spoken and written

word, because as you go up the millionaire ladder, your communications volume will skyrocket. You will need to advise, argue, debate, soothe, cajole, and convince; and you need to be able to do these while sounding courteous, firm, and knowledgeable; and all at the same time.

People overlook this very basic skill, and if you need help to shore up your communication skills, consider Toastmasters' for oral speaking, and search for writing courses or materials online.

If you are high up enough on the millionaire chain to hire writers and editors, you need to be smart on how to use them. Your written output needs to be congruent with how you speak, and what you speak of. It is just as bad to have a disconnect between your persona on a paper.

Millionaires are masters in getting their point across in the shortest and simplest means possible. They speak in precise and concise terms, yet every one of their sentences possesses deep meaning and substance. Using a lot of words and using big words are needless and just project pomposity and even insecurity.

You do not want your audience to nod off and feel like they need to consult a dictionary for every other sentence that you speak. You can turn off people, and maybe eliminate opportunities if people turn around and give up on what you should say. Keep it short and sweet.

8 - Habits with Your Body

When one sees Mark Cuban, Larry Ellison, or even Richard Branson, it is apparent that they appear to have reached the pinnacles of their success because of their health or they got to their chiseled looks because they had the billions to do so. But for every hunky looking kazillionaire, there is a dowdy Bill Gates or Warren Buffet that look like they have never spent a minute of their lives in the weight room.

It turns out that the rich and super rich are just as disciplined with their diet and exercise as they are with working and carrying out their passions. Interviews and studies with the top billionaires including those we just mentioned revealed that the super-rich exercise almost every day, and have very restrictive diets, shunning bad fats, lots of sweets.

Some, as in the case of President Donald Trump take no alcohol. But exercise is a common denominator. A focused study on millionaires revealed that 80% of wealthy people exercise every day.

These people know that they need a healthy vessel to be able work effectively to carry out their passions. They make sure that their body is in peak condition to augment their hyperactive brains.

The Sweat Habits

This is different from the sweat that we shed when we talked about exercise. In this section, sweat is about how we work and conduct business on a daily basis.

That is why the Passion Habit is so important – because if we really love and are passionate about what we like to do with our lives and in our work, working up the sweat to accomplish our goals would not even be an issue. Millionaires act in a certain way and you should do too.

Millionaires rise and shine early!

If you poll 1,000 millionaires from anywhere around the United States, there would be an excellent chance that at least 99% of them does not sleep past 8 a.m. in the morning. A great majority of these 1,000 are up by six in the morning while most of the rest of the world have not yet even gotten up for their morning shower or breakfast.

Boxing great Muhammad Ali would wake up before daybreak to start jogging and get his body in shape. When he was preparing to fight George Foreman in Zaire, he was running as if his life depended on it because he knows that his ensuing "rope a dope" strategy would require a lot of stamina.

Waking up before everybody else gives competitive people a feeling that they are gaining an edge on their opponents, who they know are still in their most unproductive mode: sleeping.

CEO's Tim Cook of Apple, Dan Akerson of General Motors, Robert Iger of Disney, and Howard Schultz of Starbucks are all up by 5:00 in the morning all ready for their work day. They may not be up and about writing memos or barking orders to their staff, but their minds are already activated, all raring to get started.

This habit arises mostly from the passion that these people have for their craft. The adrenaline coursing through their body their just will not allow them to keep their bodies in a horizontal position for extended periods of time. Waking up early is a habit that is definitely something that most passionate millionaires do not need to bother to do for 66 days consciously, because they will just do it anyway.

If you are not an early riser anyway, you do not need to wake up two or three hours before your regular waking hours just for the sake of emulating the uber successful millionaires.

You need enough sleep to be productive during the day and sufficient sleep is a must. If you can get yourself to wake up at least half an hour every day to plan and review and revisit your goals, it may explode your progress to unimaginable levels.

Ask questions

It is easy to assume that successful millionaires are too proud to admit that they do not have complete knowledge to any and all aspects of their business or job. While a vast majority of millionaires and millionaires are stubborn and headstrong, they are also an intensely curious and inquisitive bunch, which speaks to their passion to know as much about their craft as possible.

Most of us assume that we know the answers to most questions. This is a dangerous assumption that can actually hold you back from millionaire success. You should always seek clarification and direction when you begin to doubt anything about your goals.

Most people would rather guess than be "exposed" to having inadequate knowledge as if this were a mortal personality flaw. The other reason people fail to ask is that they fear that questioning may lead to further questions and further laborious thinking and analysis.

Voltaire, the genius French philosopher said, "Judge a man by his questions rather than his answers."

If you want to be successful, don't be afraid to question, ask them, but be careful not to answer your own questions. In fact, you should question your answers to yourself if you failed to consult other people.

Listen more and talk less

Actively listening means not just hearing other people talk, but listening to the essence of what people are saying. People think their listening skills are above average, just as most think that they are smarter than the average person.

In actuality, very few people actually know how to listen properly. Millionaires listen because they truly want to know as much as they can and mine other people's brains for additional insight and knowledge. Who do they listen to? Everyone – customers, vendors, bosses, and subordinates.

The proper way to listen is to focus and at the outset, put away your gadget or your phone. Use positive body language to keep the other person wired in and interested in you and what you are talking. Try to keep your mouth shut while listening, and reserve your judgment after your conversation is over.

Practice active or reflective listening. This is almost like paraphrasing what is told to you, so you can use the information more intelligently. But before getting up to wrap up the meeting, ask good questions AFTER the other people have said their piece.

If you fail to listen properly, you may miss out on some key information that you may need for your business.

Don't procrastinate and avoid "time wasters"

This is usually not an issue for millionaires consumed by their passion. But this is a no-brainer nonetheless. Time is the millionaire's most important resource because spent time cannot be recovered – once it is spent it is gone.

Sometimes, spending time to do unimportant and even irrelevant things is just another way to procrastinate. Don't spend 30 minutes talking on the phone with a supplier or customer by talking about last night's game winning home run, or your wife's tuna casserole recipe.

In the movie Wall Street, the character Gordon Gecko says, "Lunch is for wimps," echoing what most masters of the universe feel about the one hour or so spent acquiring mid-day food. You don't necessarily need to miss your meals, but avoid other unnecessary time wasters.

Even while at home, relaxation can be adjusted to make your time productive. For example, unless it can be medically proven that television is good for you, try to cut watching television time by at least half. Surveys have shown that around 2/3 of successful millionaires watch less than one hour of television daily. There are very good reasons why it is called the idiot box.

Even internet use can be a big time-waster, even if technology is such an important factor in your millionaire life. Those same studies show that over 60% of successful millionaires spend less than an hour daily surfing the net for content not related to their work or business.

These wealthy people use the time that they would have spent in surfing the net or surfing with a TV remote on personal development and education, their other income streams, networking, and even volunteering. As your passion heats up as your sweat habits improve, this may eventually take care of itself, as you may just switch off leisurely TV and internet surfing on your own.

The flipside of the TV and internet statistics are revealing: Almost 80% of people who consider themselves to be struggling financially spend an hour or more a day on those "leisurely" activities.

Make decisions and quickly

Making quick decisions decisively – that is a hallmark of a successful millionaire. The more decisions are made, the more successful a person seems to be. This goes with the responsibility territory also, since the more responsibilities and power you get, you get more questions and requests, and you need to make a lot more decisions.

While a typical person can make ten inconsequential decisions per day – where to eat, whether to take the car or the bus, etc., successful millionaires make hundreds,

Decisions made by the wealthy affect the lives of many other people – employees, customers, investors, vendors, etc. If you make the most decisions, you will win even if your decisions do not lead to good results. What would you do if you decided to drive into the opposite direction of a one-way street?

You made a mistake, but you must make quick decisions and adjustments to avert disaster. There is that other word: Quick. Sometimes, delayed action is just as bad or worse than no action at all. Successful millionaires often must make decisions on the fly, and because they do, it sets them apart from the rest.

Quick decision-making also reflects a lack of fear and the willingness to take on risk. Every uber rich success has taken a big risk in their road to riches. If you do not take the untraveled road, you may forfeit the opportunities at the end of that road.

You need to decide even it will lead you into uncharted or dangerous waters. The answers, good or bad, will come anyway, and you either learn from your mistakes or strike it rich.

Never mention the words, "bad luck" when it comes to results

Bad luck is the result of an accumulation of seemingly small bad habits that turn into disasters. They are like seemingly harmless snowflakes that accumulate like a solid mountain on a clogged driveway – they can cause massive destruction if left unchecked.

Celebrity chef Gordon Ramsay talked about how his gourmet restaurants suffered over a 1/3 decline in sales during and immediately after the 2008 financial disaster. He never mentioned the words "bad luck" even if the financial tsunami that hit his business had nothing to do with anything he did.

It helped that he had built a strong enough business to withstand the drop in sales, and instead of regretting his bad luck, worked twice as hard by changing menus, doubling his marketing efforts, and made sure he hired the best people.

In a job, bad luck is a very bad excuse to give for missing deadlines or making serious mistakes. Proper preparation and focus prevents what mortals perceive as bad luck from happening.

Do not blame others

Blaming others for missteps and disasters even if it is other people's fault is a big waste of time and energy. Constructive criticism for those at fault should not take too much time. Instead of extended periods of blame, use to time to create and implement solutions.

Blaming others also suggests that some outside influence (aside from yourself) caused a mistake or a misstep and it takes time and effort to try to explain these away.

Compete Only With Yourself.

To excel in whatever millionaire enterprise you are in, you have to consider yourself as your number one competition. If you are not leading the pack, the view from the rear will never change unless you do something about yourself. You cannot do anything about what your competition does except to become better and outsell or outperform them.

You should not imitate, you should innovate. It is okay to be knowledgeable about your competition, but you cannot allow this awareness to swallow all your attention. If you keep on watching where others are going, you may lose sight of your own direction.

If you work in an office, don't be obsessed with what your peers are doing, because you can easily descend to comparing yourself along petty lines: clothes, cars, gadgets, relationships. Be the best that you can be, and let your results make other people decide on your merits.

Control your emotions, and once again, PMA!

Emotions of fear, anger, doubt, and envy unfortunately translate into unsavory words leaving your mouth. The first course to take is to try to say as little as possible (even via email or memo) when you feel that emotions are overwhelming you.

Not every thought needs to be verbally expressed or written. When you unloose your lips for non-essential venting, you not only risk hurting others, but you will certainly hurt yourself and your prospects.

A study once determined that 70% of those who are openly expressive of their emotions struggle financially, while 95% of rich people keep their mouths in check. Count to 10, or even wait hours or a day before you say what's on your mind so you can clear your mind for some objective assessment.

The second course of action is to keep the emotions in check in the first place, so you don't have to worry checking what you say. This is where a positive mental attitude, PMA, enters the picture again.

Fear is the hardest emotion to keep a lid on, because even seemingly happy events can trigger fear, like getting 1,000 new customers (How do we service all of them?), or being assigned a difficult career-making project (How can I even handle this on top of everything else?)

Successful millionaires are conditioned to overcome negative thoughts and even ignore them. This is the best approach, and PMA is the tool for it. Turn difficulties into opportunities which most of the time they are, and don't even consider failure as an outcome, much less an option.

Review your performance each night

It is widely known that we learn more from our mistakes than from what we do right. In companies, manufacturing, accounting and human resources departments hum along quietly and nicely until a mistake happens, then all hell breaks loose.

Departmental reviews, weekend retreats, and annual assessments are made to see what has transpired, and how things can be made better. Successful people however, do not wait for these events before they figure out what went wrong and what went right because they want to take remedial and corrective action immediately.

Doing an end-of the day review is not only millionaire-smart, it is essential. There is no time to wait for mistakes to be rectified, and certainly no time before you can create opportunities to replicate your successes. Go to sleep every night knowing that you have learned a lot more about yourself and your millionaire endeavors.

9 - Habits with Your Pocketbook

Most people look at millionaire successes and visualize men and women in fur bathrobes opening the gold-plated spigot in their marble bathrooms that pour out an endless fountain of hundred-dollar bills.

Because of passion, skill, and just plain hard work, millionaires know how to make money. They have also developed habits that make them keep their money and make their money grow. Their habits are simple but for most. difficult to do.

Discipline is in itself a habit and money discipline is what makes millionaires, and keeps them that way. The following millionaire habits have been observed in practically every self-made millionaire.

Pay yourself first

The surest way to get to millions is to make sure that when you collect money from your business or employer, put aside a portion of it first before you use the money to spend on anything else. This "tithing" habit ensures that a portion of your income goes into savings, which you can use for future investment, retirement, or unforeseen emergencies.

Nothing can be worse that to end up empty handed when you need the money most. Unfunded emergencies can be catastrophic from a financial point of view if you do not have the proper buffers to protect against them.

This habit comes along with being able to live within your means. Millionaires dull the propensity to overspend by putting aside a big chunk of their income into accounts that they cannot easily convert to spendable cash. Most put away at least 20% of their income, and "live" on whatever is left.

Don't spend what you don't have

Most Americans are stuck in what financial advisers call the "Income Trap." They spend whatever they get right away, instead of paying themselves first before thinking of saving for a rainy day.

Christmas and mid-year bonuses from work, inheritances, and other windfalls are spent after they've barely touched a bank account. They have already thought of a luxury vacation, a new gadget, or a new wardrobe. After spending all of it, they acquire a taste of the good stuff and turn to their credit cards to keep the spending machine going.

This one-day millionaire mindset will prevent you from becoming a millionaire. The outlook of "living life to the fullest" is dangerous for financial stability, because "one-time, good-time" thinking can give you a false feeling of security.

You need to accept the reality that you will probably not win the lottery or have another relative die on you to leave you a lot of cash. We need to look at the other side of the world to see how it's done sometimes.

Most Chinese people in Asia have an aversion for credit. Their financial success especially outside China is bookended by their frugality and keen business sense. The miserly ways of the very rich and successful Chinese are legend in those parts. They delay their gratification for luxuries and non-essentials, and will only spend for those after they have saved enough to splurge.

Ethnic Chinese in Malaysia, Singapore and Indonesia are known to spend most of their lives working and saving, and cumulatively, the results speak for themselves. While they are the minority population in some countries, they control a significant proportion of the monetary assets of those countries.

Accumulating huge savings meant that they could establish

and fund banks, factories, and all sorts of major businesses. More importantly, the delayed gratification means that not only can they provide adequately for their descendants, and they can have a comfortable and even luxurious life when in matters most – at an age where they can appreciate the fruits of financial freedom.

A famous millionaire once excoriated middle-class America, and blamed the media for their spending habits. He said that most middle-class folks seek instant gratification. At your earning years, you should be seeking comfort and not freedom; freedom which will come when you have accumulated enough money to do what you want.

This doesn't mean that you will be a failure if your savings from the delay of gratification do not lead to you building up a big, successful business. Having a million dollars in your bank account at a certain age can feel just as satisfying.

This also doesn't mean that everyone should forego a $7.00 Latte whenever they feel like it or wait for movies to come out on DVD to save on movie tickets. You don't have to deprive yourself to a monastic existence to do this habit. Just keep the mindset that it is unnatural to give away what you don't own.

Chinese people love to gamble. The difference between most gamblers and an overwhelming majority of Chinese gamblers is that Chinese put aside a portion of their saved money just precisely for this otherwise futile endeavor (This can be a quick tip: create an entertainment budget from which gambling money can be used.)

For some of us with a gambling compunction and no big savings account to dip into, gambling is a losing bet. Almost 80% if those who struggle financially actually play the lottery for that one big windfall. Successful millionaires do not rely on "good luck" and stratospheric odds for their wealth. They simply create their own good luck.

Try to avoid personal credit as much as you can

Credit is an excellent way to expand a business. You would gladly pay 10% interest a year to have the see a bigger version of your business return at least twice as much. For businesses, credit used in the right way is an unassailable business decision. For individuals, however, the only reason to get personal credit is to make sure that you have it.

This sounds like a circular argument, but put another way,

credit is an excellent facility to have, but a dangerous one nevertheless. It is like an ancient army defending a fort: You have people sitting on barrels of gunpowder which is absolutely necessary for your survival during a crunch; but potentially, can blow up under your noses if not properly handled.

Long-time consumer advice show host Clark Howard avoided this gunpowder keg altogether and hit a road block when his credit score fell precipitously because he used absolutely no credit, even buying his house for cash.

It is good to have a credit card, charge on it, but make sure you pay off the balance it total when the bill comes due. We all know of the horror stories of people who run up mountains of credit card debt, only to find out that they can only pay the minimum required balances each month.

The problem is that for most people, this is a dangerous habit. They use their credit card for everything, put down a little, and make tiny payments on the balance, the minimum payments. It takes a long time to settle debt like this. About 40 years to pay off a credit card if you make only minimum payments on it.

A corollary to this habit is to make sure that you keep your credit score as high as possible. Make it a habit to check your credit score periodically, using one of the more reputable credit monitoring services.

Create multiple streams of income

On a large scale, big companies diversify into other lines of business to stay relevant but mostly to increase their income streams. Walmart started selling fresh groceries with some success; on the flipside, Microsoft expanded into a few ill-advised ventures such as their music player and cellphones.

Many self-made millionaires that are not on the Walmart or Microsoft scale do not rely on only a single source of income. For the passionate office worker who works really hard, his single income from a fixed salary may not be enough to reach that million dollar mark.

So making a million may sometimes require take one source of income. It seems that the average number of streams of income of millionaires is three. Why do you need more than one stream? This is mostly to create a buffer against uncertainties such as economic downturns and job layoffs.

Supplemental streams of income can come from stock market investments, annuities, real estate rentals, multi-network marketing, and even part ownership in other side businesses.

Invest and invest wisely - don't let the money sit around

You need to view investment and savings as two completely different pools of your hard-earned, unspent money. Saved money should never be subject to too much speculation, and should be shielded from losses, because they will be used for emergencies.

Six months' worth of salaries or living expenses is the typical savings level that most financial advisers give. This presupposes that you will need six months to get a new job, or get a business back up in earning condition. Beware, however, because you should be very judicious in selecting the proper savings vehicle.

Millionaires will not leave their money in a bank savings account earning one-half of one percent interest annually. They work hard for their money, so in return they make their money work for them.

Many people want to be ultra-conservative with their

money and insist on the financial equivalent of leaving their money inside a mattress - they leave the money in bank savings accounts or money market funds that earn minuscule interest rates significantly less than the inflation rate. If prices go up an average of 3% a year, and your money grows at ½ of 1%, you are losing a lot of ground.

People were spooked during the 2008 financial crises, when supposedly solid institutions like Lehman Brothers and Washington Mutual Bank were liquidated. Many people lost their investments and retirement accounts, and money flowed into precious metals and those savings accounts.

A vast majority of successful millionaires work hard to take care of the money that they in turn, worked hard to earn. They take tax reduction and risk very seriously in doing so. In a financial survey, over half of them believe that taxes, or minimizing them, are a bigger consideration than the actual returns that they get from an investment.

A majority have admitted that while they are mavericks and daredevils in their fields of expertise, they are also generally risk-averse. They find it hard to contemplate a scenario where their hard-earned money can disappear because they did not factor in risk enough.

But when you accumulate a lot of money over several years, you need to diversify your investments. Many millionaires invest conventionally. At least 80% of millionaires invest in stocks and bonds which help them accumulate much higher gains than just leaving them in bank savings accounts.

If you are an employee, contribute as much as you can to your company's retirement plan, especially a 401K or 403b employer sponsored plan. Contributions to the plan are made pre-tax so that your tax liabilities are minimized because your contributions are deducted from your gross pay. Most companies also match part or even, all your contributions, so your savings can grow much faster.

Share Your Millions

Giving away money is always a win-win situation. Wealthy millionaires practice blessed giving – they believe that there is a time for contribution, after a significant amount of accumulation. They bless others with part of what they have been given with open hearts. Wealthy people of have given away money seem to have much more come back to them eventually.

The rich practice the principle of blessed giving. They share what they have with open hearts. Giving is a money multiplier that adds value to their prosperity in multiples. In 2012, when Facebook founder Mark Zuckerberg was worth an estimated $17 billion dollars according to Forbes Magazine, he gave away close to half a billion ($499 million) dollars to charity.

The giving didn't hurt him, in 2017, Forbes Magazine estimated his net worth to be around $56 billion, a jump of over 200% since he gave away what at the time seemed a huge chunk of his fortune.

The results are about the same for the uber wealthy such as mega contributors Bill Gates and Warren Buffet, who have seen their individual net worth increase over and beyond what they have contributed for charitable causes. Gates has given away around 50 billion dollars ever since his net worth was estimated at around $10 billion. In 2017, Forbes Magazine estimated his wealth to be around $86 billion.

Why does giving pay you back in spades? There is no other plausible explanation but maybe, good karma. Maybe there is something to Rhonda Byrnes' The Secret and the Law of Attraction: If you give up positive vibes while you are giving away your money, the Universe will return it back to you with a lot of interest!

Habits with Your Networks and People

Working with other people is an essential part of any success story. Walmart founder Sam Walton had to drive millions of miles over his life to talk to suppliers, visit possible store sites, and (sometimes incognito) talking to customers and employees at his stores.

Unless you have developed some sort of killer app where you can earn millions just by churning out algorithms from a deserted island, you probably need to work with other people to realize your millionaire success story. It will be you working with other people that will determine whether you will be a millionaire success.

"Networking" for a millionaires can send up visions of white-gloved waiters walking around offering champagne and canapes, or in a low-brow version, singing karaoke with their friends to rub elbows with prospective clients and customers. People print out a ton of business cards and hand them out indiscriminately over an evening hoping to bag the big fish.

Millionaires, however, mostly ignore or skip these events that they consider frivolous and a waste of their time. They believe that networking is not really working, so it subtracts and detracts from real productive time.

Most people just starting out make the mistake of spending more time on networking "events" than on their businesses. Successful millionaires are discerning about what events to attend. Instead of building a stack of business cards, they are building their businesses or sharpening their work skills.

But since these can be valuable opportunities to mingle with others that you do not regularly socialize with (such as office parties, where you can get to hobnob with your bosses), they can be tolerated for a few choice instances.

But do not think for a moment that millionaires are generally, or should be, loners. Most of them, are in fact, social butterflies. They are constantly chatting up new people and meeting with anyone and everyone who are interested in their business or job.

They put in a lot of work into widening their network and acknowledge that successful relationships are the key to millions. Business people have their favorite bankers and financiers, authors their agents and publishers, and employees their "backers" and company mentors. They are just very selective in how they create and cultivate these networks.

While you can attend a few cocktail parties just to be "seen" and be relevant in their industries or jobs, networking as a millionaire habit means much more than giving out business cards to a bunch of people. Networking should be seen as marketing events, where you the rest of the world can see you as a unique product.

Consider yourself a brand and make yourself into one

"A brand is a promise delivered." This famous advertising mantra is applicable in products and in millionaire success.

We know what branding is on a business level: Kleenex. Coca-Cola, BMW are all well-known and "trusted" brands. Consumers buy things because they know that trust a certain brand because quality and reliability. A brand can be a name, a symbol, a person, a design, or a sound. It can also be employees, reputation, and even tone and emotion.

One of the most important characteristics of a brand is that it separates the "product" from other similar products. The golden arches of McDonald's is such an iconic symbol, with the golden letter "M" recognizable even to young children who have even yet started learning the alphabet. Now you yourself must become a brand with the same effectiveness as the McDonald's "M".

Effective branding is the key to business success, but it is now just as important on your personal level, and is a must if you want to achieve millionaire success. Building a personal brand can lead to a ton of professional opportunities including industry recognition, better customers and vendors, and a better, higher-paying job. Proper branding will extend your reach and expose you to a much wider audience.

Before you network, you must make sure that what you are putting out there is an image that is admired and that it attracts positive attention – it should be a brand that can be "marketed". This is the number one priority in networking – you do not want to market a crummy product, you, in the first place.

There is added emphasis on personal branding today because of the internet and the explosion of social media. Employers have been increasingly placing their reliance on social media to screen job applicants before even seeing them.

It is easy to Google an applicant and look at their Facebook and LinkedIn profiles, for example to see what they are all about. Search engines are the first layers of character and reference checks.

10 - So what do you do to build a personal brand?

Make sure your reputation is intact and respectable. It may be hard to create a brand if you have led a Charles Manson-like existence, but for most people, it means living a clean life free of controversy, or scrubbing past missteps with subsequent acts of retribution and "cleansing."

Define yourself as a specialty or specialist within a field, product range, or expertise. For example, more than being associated with an apple or computers, Steve Jobs and Bill Gates have forever been linked to cutting edge computer technology. If you are an employee looking for a big payday, can prospective employers consider you as a must-have with your education, training, and specialized experience?

You need to project consistency and stability. If you are associated with computers, you don't want to be associated with fruits and vegetables after a couple of years. It is like seeing your professional affiliation as an actuary in 2010, and being a hairstyling guru in 2017. Be a one-product, or one-service product, so potential "buyers" can see a commitment to excellence, expertise, consistency, and quality.

If you are seeking to increase revenues, you want potential customers to link your name with a sense of long-term success, satisfaction, and trust. Some people like Steve Jobs not only let the apple be a symbol of his enterprise, but he always showed up in public events in his trademark jeans and turtleneck. While wardrobe consistency is not a must, the consistency mind set should be.

Find a mentor

An overwhelming percentage of successful, self-made millionaires credit their riches and success to having mentors. It is a potential fast track to success and riches that is will be one of the least painful. Surprisingly, they may be also easy to find, and will not cost any significant investment to do so.

The first place to look for mentors is within your own family circles. Parents are an important source of direction and advice, because they really are a person's first mentors. On the winding, bumpy and sometimes lofty path to success, they can provide the "grounding" to make sure that you retain your values. Don't ignore your siblings, uncles, aunts, grandparents and so forth.

These people know you best, and may have a lot of great insight on your strengths, potential, and limitations. A key in a good mentorship relationship is to establish one that is long-term in nature where your mentors can watch your progress from start to finish, so that they can advise in the context of your overall growth.

Professors and even your teachers from your youth can provide some needed guidance at both technical and personal levels. Your university professor in your chosen field is an excellent resource not only because of the specialized technical knowledge, but also because

Co-workers and bosses, even former ones have been invaluable to successful millionaires. They have specific knowledge of your field, and can also help your advancement by bending the ear of people that have a say in handing out promotions. To truly realize the benefits of these mentors, seek out a mentor who is at least two levels or positions above your own.

Industry figures, even if you do not work directly with them will provide specific expert advice on your specific field.

Aside from being experts in your field, a critical quality that you need to find in a mentor is that they must be able to dispense harsh and critical commentary without being afraid of hurting your feelings.

You can advise them of this up front, or you can simple discern from their tone if they don't mind being brutally open and frank. They should strike a balance between objectivity and fairness with genuineness and compassion.

You will also want a mentor that is genuinely curious and concerned about your progress. They should be inquisitive and constantly be asking questions about your path to your millions. A mentor that just nods yes to everything you say is a waste of time.

Eventually, you may want to develop a mentorship circle, or a brain trust, whose membership is limited to those whose knowledge, opinions, and advice you can completely trust and rely on. You want to keep it to a small and compact group so that you can easily distill their collective knowledge to a coherent body of work.

Consider advice and information from anyone

While you mostly want to have lofty networking contacts, you should not reject or shrug off inputs from people wholesale. A study once showed that 95% of CEOs asked their lowest level employees for their opinions on how to run their businesses.

It is because these employees usually have the closest contacts to customers and vendors. They may also have unfound brilliance simmering inside just waiting to be discovered, like a rough diamond encased in tons of earth and dirt. You will never know what they know if you do not ask.

Zhou Qunfei, currently China's richest woman was a mere factory worker in a company making watch face glass. After the company went bankrupt, she used the concept of the watch face glass to make glass faces for cell phones and computers. Imagine what would have happened if her employer had interviewed her and asked her how his business could be much better and bigger?

Ultimately, the people that you truly need to be networking with will not be the schmoozers found at typical networking socials. While you strive to always network at your level, you should not ignore the "smaller" guy.

Associate with successful people, and avoid toxic people

Successful millionaires remind us that we are only as successful as the people that we mingle with. A survey found out that 90% of successful millionaires associate with the like kind of people. On the other hand, over 95% of people who struggle financially regularly associate with people who also have financial issues.

As much as possible, you should network with people above your level. Most of your networking activities should be done with people with stronger resume's, longer and more varied experience, and much higher positions than yours.

Just as a chess player can only get better by playing against much tougher competition, you should expose yourself to people that are already very successful in your field so that you can mine the best minds.

But this does not necessarily mean that all successful people are candidates that we should hang around with. There are jerks, malcontents, and misanthropes among the rich and very rich, and we do not want whatever they have to rub off on us. There are many rich and successful people who are negative and dispense destructive criticism all the time.

Associating with these people can derail your progress. Instead, you would want to hang around those people who possess an abundance of PMA, are enthusiastic, optimistic, goal-oriented, tireless, and have unquestionable integrity and honesty.

You may want to divvy up your associations between "Rich Relationships" and "Poor Relationships". You evaluate each of your relationships and classify them either as someone who can help you in your climb up the millionaire ladder, or someone who will hold you back.

You do not necessarily have to cut ties with your poor relationships (poor Uncle Frank who can't even keep a nickel in his pocket) but you can minimize your contact with them. Rich relationships lead you to better contacts, a new job, new doors of opportunity, and business referrals.

Invest resources in productive and success-oriented people.

If you have the power to hire and fire, or have the clout an employee to choose those who can and can't work for you, consider yourself really blessed. In the same way that a business person invests in productive and money making physical assets like factories and computers, you should always pay attention to, and consider paying for productive human assets.

The amount of time attention and energy that you pour into

productive and successful people will multiply your own successes.

These people can be "cultivated" in a variety of ways where the will feel that they are not only appreciated, but needed: Just calling to say hello every day; greeting them on an important event or milestone like a birthday or anniversary (Lay it on thick and include their spouses and children); and ask them on social functions and brainstorming sessions reserved for "very special people."

This point should be reiterated: Networking IS NOT socializing, and should never be viewed or approached like it is. Only go to networking events if there is a prospect of interacting with the powerful and influential people in your field. Temper this with the attitude that not everyone who attends these events are a true resource worth spending time on.

11 - Habits with your Communications and Technology

The business world has been taken over almost completely by technology. There is almost no aspect of the road to millions that is not touched by the internet and automation. More millionaires are being created through technology than almost any other field or business. After financial investing and stocks, technology has become the second most common way to create millionaire fortunes.

This is no surprise given that the sheer speed and scale wherein new internet technologies can spread and touch almost anyone worldwide can be a powerful tool for you to create riches in a manner that was not possible even just thirty years ago.

Using the internet does not necessarily mean that you need to have a technology- or internet-based product to make your millions. In your millionaire voyage, using the internet is an essential tool in whatever endeavor you are pursuing, whether you are in business or in employment.

Start a blog or a website

If you don't have a tech presence, get one immediately. To start a blog or website does not take a whole lot of money or effort.

If you don't have the tech expertise, pay for it.

The internet has been considered the great "equalizer" for many areas in daily life. In journalism, the old "paper-based" periodicals, built on billions of dollars of investments over a hundred years have mostly fallen into the dustbin of irrelevancy.

News coverage and especially opinions, once the exclusive enclave of the major print media, can now be engaged in by almost anybody with access to the internet and the most basic of equipment and software.

Where it used to take millions of dollars to locate, identify, and contact prospective customers, all it takes today is a free Facebook account to do exactly the thing. The list goes on with other business endeavors, from research to accounting to taxes – computers and the World Wide Web are taking over more and more of typical business functions.

Many people can be lulled by the increasing ease by which people can use various tools in the internet. Posting pictures, writing product descriptions, and even creating rudimentary websites can be made by people who haven't even graduated from high school.

This can work for those who are part-time users of the internet with no aspirations to becoming a millionaire. For those however, who are thinking of building empires, professionalism is a must.

Start with appearances. If you have a website, hire a professional to design a snazzy looking website that has immediate eye appeal. If you repel the most casual viewer, you will not generate any traffic.

Going deeper, you may also hire a content writer or editor to make sure that your website gets the directed traffic and exposure it needs. There are many other skills that you may want to outsource, and your needs will depend on your product, your funding, and what your website objectives are,

Outside of a website, fill in your knowledge gap in ancillary activities like accounting and human resources with cloud- or internet based applications. The good news about a lot of the better products is that they are scalable, and can "grow" with you. Get help when you need it because you should devote your time to growing your business and improving your product or service.

12 - Audit your online presence

If you are an employee looking to move on to much greater and better things, knowing your overall online profile is invaluable knowledge. When we talked about networking, we established that more than ever, employers are using search engines to do their background search on prospective employees.

You cannot afford not to know what you can look like to your target employers. You need to use search engines as your primary tool to do this.

The first thing to look for is whether you have social media accounts that were created by other people pretending to be you. You should be prepared to report these immediately to the security personnel of whatever social media site that included the bogus account. Many times, a duplicate account on the same social media platform can be created maliciously for whatever malevolent reason.

The second thing you need to do is to "scrub" your accounts for unsavory profiles or information that may compromise your chances for landing a great opportunity. Delete any accounts in any sites that some employers may find illicit or immoral.

These could be adult chat or dating websites, or groups espousing violence or other issues that may be controversial or out of the mainstream. Scrubbing also means refining your current social media profiles to remove any unsavory references.

Lastly, you should scour your accounts for any inconsistencies between your various accounts. Basic information such as birth dates, birth places, residence, educational information, jobs and timelines should be consistent between social media platforms. There are free websites and apps that help you identify what sites you are in, so you can revisit and updated when needed.

Look for yourself in search engines on a regular basis, and set up alerts for each time your name is recorded on the internet. This may be a challenge for very common names, and differentiation can take a lot of work but the effort will be well worth it.

13 - Conclusion

After all this, do you have what it takes to be a millionaire? We have talked about taking a small step each time, and in 66 days turning some step into a habit makes you move up to the bigger picture: You create a process of success.

Think of the process to make smooth and silky butter. It includes the less than elegant steps of shepherding a cow into a muddy stall, pulling the teats for milk that splashes around, leading up to the steps of churning the dairy product amidst all the heat and the noise of the butter factory.

Create the success process

More than processing a tangible product or money, what millionaires process is success. Success is the culmination and accumulation of the groups of effective habits that we have just discussed.

When these habits have jelled together in 66 days or however many days it takes, it creates a process that is almost automatic, and eliminates a counterproductive thinking process that uses up a lot of time and energy. By creating the millionaire success habits, we do not need to THINK about WHAT to do, WHY we need to do it, HOW to do it, and the doubt-creating WHAT HAPPENS if we did it? We can now use our brains for something else!

Do not fear failure and criticism

Inherent to the success process is the need to have some sort of feedback mechanism that tells us how we did, how we can correct what went wrong, and how we can replicate the amazing things that were accomplished. This is where the ability to receive criticism comes in.

The feedback process is essential and a proper process of receiving and processing feedback is a required success habit. Successful millionaires welcome criticism because they understand that it is crucial for growth and learning.

It provides the information, motivation, and purpose to experiment and even change course. An employee may decide that he would want another career in the same company, or be in an all new profession together.

A company can add or drop product lines, and open or close factories and offices all in the name of future success. None of this is possible if you cannot accept criticism, or fear the consequences of corrective action.

Erase all doubt

Over 80% of successful millionaires attribute their success to their beliefs, and their belief in themselves. Most of them mention names like success gurus Dale Carnegie, Jim Rohn, and Dale Carnegie.

Whether in business or employment, forget all the self-limiting thoughts that have held back your success. You probably have heard it all before: Money begets money, so the poor cannot become rich; Rich people have all the luck (and maybe the genetics), you're not smart or educate enough; you have failed everything that you've ever tried.

Be congruent and consistent

In the same way that you need to be consistent with in your online presence, you need to be consistent in whatever you do or say. First, you must say what you are going to do. You want people to see you as determined and committed. Second, and more important, is that what you do should not be in opposition to your personal values and beliefs.

Even if you face a lot of resistance, you will be respected by everyone. Not every millionaire success story who won with integrity and honesty is liked, but you can be damned sure they are respected, and that is what really matters.

Become a master

Successful millionaires never thought about settling for second best. Their competition juices will not allow them to be upstaged by competition. This means that they should know more, and know how to do things better than anyone in their field. They will absorb and process all possible inputs that they can gather around them and use the to their advantage.

The best golfers in the world practice 50 putts all day to make sure that the 8-foot ones become mere tap-ins. The really good ones stretch the boundaries of what they can do to master their craft and their business and still they know it is not enough. You need to be the unassailable leader in your field, if you want your millions.

Go above and beyond!

Finally, know your limits and then exceed them. I am sure you have heard some misdirected individual in an office say, "that's not in my job description" or even, "that's beyond my pay grade."

The result is they are rarely given any additional responsibilities and their career advancement is non-existent. Successful go getters do not worry about job descriptions. They do whatever it is that needs to get done and then some.

Wealthy people make themselves invaluable to their employees and customers. Successful millionaires strive to come up with better products, more reliable service, and a reason for customers and bosses to come back.

At some point in their lives, billionaires like Elon Musk of Tesla and Richard Branson of Virgin Airways must have been told, "the sky's the limit.!" This was not supposed to be taken literally, but it probably challenged them to the point that they wanted to be among the first entrepreneurs to make space travel a commercial enterprise.

They know what the sky is because they've reached it. What they will never stop trying to do is go beyond the blue sky towards the unending possibilities beyond it.

Thank You

As we reach the end of this book, I want to say thanks for reading this book.

I want to get this information out to as many people as possible. If you found this book helpful, I would greatly appreciate you leaving me a review. This helps others find the book as well.

This book was self-published with the amazing help of Self-Publishing Made Easy Now! [3] . You can grab a free copy of the checklist that started my journey here: FREE Self-Publishing Checklist [4] .

[3] https://selfpublishingmadeeasynow.com/xpjv

[4] https://selfpublishingmadeeasynow.com/free_checklist

Disclaimer

This document is geared towards providing exact and reliable information in regards to the topic and issue covered. The publication is sold on the idea that the publisher is not required to render an accounting, officially permitted, or otherwise, qualified services. If advice is necessary, legal, financial, medical or professional, a practiced individual in the profession should be ordered.

This information is not presented by a financial or medical practitioner and is for entertainment, educational and informational purposes only. The content is not intended as a substitute for professional medical advice, diagnosis, or treatment. Always seek the advice of your physician or other qualified health care provider with any questions you may have regarding a medical condition. Never disregard professional medical advice or delay in seeking it because of something you have read.

The information provided herein is stated to be truthful and consistent, in that any liability, in terms of inattention or otherwise, by any usage or abuse of any policies, processes, or directions contained within is the solitary and utter responsibility of the recipient reader. Under no circumstances will any legal responsibility or blame be held against the publisher for any reparation, damages, or monetary loss due to the information herein, either directly or indirectly.